DISCOVERING YOUR

IDENTITY

BY

CHARLES F. STANLEY

THOMAS NELSON
Since 1798

NASHVILLE   DALLAS   MEXICO CITY   RIO DE JANEIRO

Discovering Your Identity

Charles F. Stanley

Copyright © 1999, 2008 by Charles F. Stanley

Published in Nashville, Tennessee, by Thomas Nelson, Inc.

Editing, layout, and design by Gregory C. Benoit Publishing, Old Mystic, CT

Scripture quotations are from THE NEW KING JAMES VERSION. Copyright © 1979, 1980, 1982, Thomas Nelson, Inc., Publishers.

ISBN 978-1-4185-2817-1

Printed in the United States of America

15 16 17 18 RRD 25 24 23 22 21 20 19

Contents

INTRODUCTION
A Fresh Look at Your Identity as a Believer 1

LESSON 1
You Are a Saint! 3

LESSON 2
In Christ 12

LESSON 3
Chosen by God 23

LESSON 4
Beloved Child 34

LESSON 5
Redeemed 47

LESSON 6
Heir 66

LESSON 7
Enlightened Saint 78

LESSON 8
Member of the Body 90

LESSON 9
Holy Vessel for Ministry 102

LESSON 10
God's Masterpiece 113

A Fresh Look at Your Identity as a Believer

Every person has an outlook on the world and on life—a way of looking at things, valuing things, judging things. We need to recognize that our perspective is something which we have learned. Many Christians have a wrong understanding about certain things, including the identity that we have as believers in Christ Jesus. Many Christians don't truly know who they are in Christ. They have misconceptions about why God forgives, what salvation means to our life on this earth, and who God has called them to be.

In order to gain the right perspective on our identity as believers, we need to go to the Word of God and stay there. Books on self-esteem may be helpful to some, but only if the foundation of self-identity is firmly established on what the Word of God says. The Bible is God's foremost communication on the subject of self-esteem and self-identity. It is the reference to which we must return continually to discover who we are and how we are to respond to life's situations and to other people. Our perspective is wrong any time it doesn't match up with God's eternal truth.

This book can be used by you alone or by several people in a small-group study. At various times, you will be asked to relate to the material in one of these four ways:

1. *What new insights have you gained?* Make notes about the insights that you have. You may want to record them in your Bible or in a separate journal. As you reflect back over your insights, you are likely to see how God has moved in your life.

2. *Have you ever had a similar experience?* Each of us approaches the Bible from a unique background—our own particular set of relationships and experiences. Our experiences do not make the Bible true—the Word of God is truth regardless of our opinion about it. It is important, however, to share our experiences in order to see how God's truth can be applied to human lives.

3. *How do you feel about the material presented?* Emotional responses do not give validity to the Scriptures, nor should we trust our emotions as a gauge for our faith. In small-group Bible study, however, it is good for participants to express their emotions. The Holy Spirit often communicates with us through this unspoken language.

4. *In what way do you feel challenged to respond or to act?* God's Word may cause you to feel inspired or challenged to change something in your life. Take the challenge seriously and find ways of acting upon it. If God reveals to you a particular need that He wants *you* to address, take that as "marching orders" from God. God is expecting you to *do* something with the challenge that He has just given you.

Start and conclude your Bible study sessions in prayer. Ask God to give you spiritual eyes to see and spiritual ears to hear. As you conclude your study, ask the Lord to seal what you have learned so that you will never forget it. Ask Him to help you grow into the fullness of the stature of Christ Jesus.

Again, I caution you to keep the Bible at the center of your study. A genuine Bible study stays focused on God's Word and promotes a growing faith and a closer walk with the Holy Spirit in *each* person who participates.

LESSON 1

You Are a Saint!

☙ In This Lesson ☙

Learning: WHAT EXACTLY IS A SAINT?

Growing: HOW DOES "SAINTHOOD" APPLY TO MY SELF-EVALUATION?

How do you see yourself? Do you regard yourself as a saint? Each of us acts on the basis of how we *see* ourselves. Our opinion of self directs and focuses our behavior every hour of every day. If we have a faulty self-image—which is having any self-image other than what God says about us—we behave in a way that is contrary to God's highest purposes and plan for our lives.

Having a correct self-image is important to the way that we make personal choices, deal with problems, and approach various tasks and challenges in life. A correct self-image also affects the way that we deal with other people.

Jesus taught that we are to love our neighbors *as we love ourselves.* In other words, we are to love, appreciate, value, and treat others in the same way that we love, appreciate, value, and treat ourselves. If we do *not* love ourselves in an appropriate way, we cannot love others as God wants us to love them. A healthy, God-based self-image is vital if we are going to relate to others in a truly Christlike way.

Jesus said to him, "'YOU SHALL LOVE THE LORD YOUR GOD WITH ALL YOUR HEART, WITH ALL YOUR SOUL, AND WITH ALL YOUR MIND.' This is the first and great commandment. And the second is like it: 'YOU SHALL LOVE YOUR NEIGHBOR AS YOURSELF.' On these two commandments hang all the Law and the Prophets."

—Matthew 22:37-40

✍ Why does Jesus say that loving your neighbor is like loving God? Why does He list loving God before loving others?

✍ Why does Jesus say, "love your neighbor as yourself"? Why not, "learn to love yourself, then love your neighbor the same way"?

✍ Why do "all the Law and the Prophets" "hang" from these two commandments?

The Basis for Your Sainthood

The Bible says that those who believe in Christ Jesus and who have accepted Him as their Savior are *saints*. Each of us must choose to believe what the Bible says. Do you *believe* today that you are a saint?

Being a saint is not based upon how you *feel*. Most of us do not feel like saints on any given day. Feelings come and go. What we feel is often highly unpredictable, and emotions are certainly not a basis for making decisions about one's identity. For some people, an unruly hairdo or a spilled cup of coffee can ruin a day emotionally. No—emotions are not the basis on which we conclude that we are saints.

Being a saint is not based upon how much we *understand* about sainthood. Few people can truly say that they understand fully what it means to be a follower of Christ. None of us can fully explain the mystery of why God would choose to love us, forgive us, extend mercy and grace to us, or send His Son to die for us. A finite mind can never understand the infinite wisdom and power of almighty God. No—understanding is not the basis on which we conclude that we are saints.

Being a saint is also not based upon what others say about us. People may have said to you, "Oh, you are a real saint!" when what they really mean is, "You are truly a kind person, a generous person, or a helpful person." From the biblical point of view, sainthood has nothing to do with what a person *does* in the form of good works or kind gestures. Sainthood is bestowed upon those who believe in Christ on the basis of *what Jesus Christ has done*. The opinions of others are irrelevant and of no consequence.

So what qualifies a person to be a saint? Only one thing is required: that a person accept—receive, believe, and personally embrace—the sacrificial death of Jesus Christ on the cross. Our relationship with Jesus Christ is what qualifies us to be saints. Nothing else is required.

Within the concept of sainthood, however, we find a number of other truths. What does it truly *mean* to be a saint? How do saints live out their lives? What do saints do? These are the questions that are at the heart of this Bible study. When you acknowledge that you are a saint—a believer in Jesus Christ—you are only at the starting point for discovering *who you are in Christ*.

☙ In what ways have you been relying upon others to give you a sense of self-worth or to define your identity?

☙ How do you feel about being called "a saint of God"? How do you generally think of yourself in that regard?

A "Right" Self-Esteem

We hear a great deal about self-esteem today. Countless books have been written on the subject and nearly all of them are aimed at helping a person *raise* low self-esteem to achieve a *good* self-esteem.

⸙ Too High ⸙

People tend to fall into two broad categories. First, there are some who have self-esteem that is too high. This is a relatively small percentage of people, in my opinion, especially since many of those who *act* as if they think too highly of themselves are actually masking a low self-image. The person with too-high self-esteem is arrogant and self-centered, and has no regard for others. Such a person believes that the entire universe revolves around himself. Too-high self-esteem leads a person to conclude, "I can make it on my own if everybody else will just get out of my way." This person has the "Big I syndrome."

⸙ Too Low ⸙

Second, there are those who have self-esteem that is too low. Most people look around and conclude, "I'm not good enough; I'm not capable enough; I'm not valuable; I'm worthless." They see themselves as without purpose or desirability. They cannot comprehend that another person might love them or count them as valuable, much less that God can love them.

In many cases, those with too-low self-esteem adopt a false humility—their humility is not before God but before others. They say, "I can't do what you can do; I can't succeed as much as that person can succeed; I couldn't possibly be as effective as another person in this role." In their low self-esteem they become doormats for others to walk upon, and they often are frustrated, discouraged, depressed, and without hope for their futures.

What we don't often realize about people with too-low self-esteem is that they also see the world through the filter of their own self and their own lack of ability. They are just as guilty of the "Big I syndrome" as those with too-high self-esteem.

Let nothing be done through selfish ambition or conceit, but in lowliness of mind let each esteem others better than himself.

—Philippians 2:3

❧ Notice that Paul uses "esteem" as a verb—it is something that we choose to do, not something that "just is." How does this apply to your own self-esteem?

❧ What would your own life be like if everyone you know esteemed himself to be better than others? What if everyone esteemed others as better than himself?

The Error of Comparison

There is one great error that people make, whether their self-esteem is too low or too high: they are *comparing themselves to others*. God never calls us to compare ourselves with anyone! Each of us has been given a unique, one-of-a-kind, irreplaceable purpose in God's plan. We have been created *as we are* by a loving God who wants us to fulfill the purpose that *He* has for our lives. It is when we compare ourselves to others that we say, "I'm not like that person" and then conclude, "I'm not as good" or "I'm so much better."

Comparison separates and divides us from one another, but of even greater consequence is the fact that comparison leads us to false conclusions about ourselves and, therefore, to faulty behavior. When we think that we are better than others, we treat them as inferior or as failures. When we think that we are not as valuable as others, we treat them with undue deference, resentment, and envy. Both sets of behavior keep us from loving others fully or appreciating the fullness of *who* God made them to be.

"Right" Self-Esteem

What God calls us to is neither a too-high nor a too-low self-esteem. God wants us to have a *right* self-esteem. A correct self-image can never be rooted in comparison with others. It can never be concluded on the basis of what others think about us, say to us, or even the way that we feel about ourselves. A correct self-image is based upon what *God* says about us in His Word.

Correct self-esteem is totally opposite to the "Big I" syndrome. Correct self-esteem says that I do not know myself fully—but God does. Correct self-esteem says that I cannot determine my own goodness or achieve my own forgiveness and righteousness—but I can accept what Jesus Christ has done on my behalf. Correct self-esteem concludes that I do not have the ability to love others unconditionally in my own strength—but that I can love others as God helps me to love them.

What *God* says about our identity is generally totally opposite to what the world says. The world says, "You have to make your own success." God says, "Have a relationship with Me, trust Me, and I will give you total fulfillment and satisfaction." The world says, "If you don't make your own way and proclaim your own greatness, you'll be run over or disregarded by others." God says, "The greatest among you will become the servant of all, and in that, I will be well pleased with you." The world says, "Get all you can so that you can become all you are." God says, "Give away all you can so that you can gain your own soul." God wants us to look to *Him* for our self-definition and for our identity.

Perhaps the most important question that we can ask ourselves at the outset of this study is this: *To whom am I looking for my self-identity, my self-image, my self-worth?* Are you relying on your parents? Many people are still listening to "old tapes" of what their parents said to them when they were children. Some of those tapes are faulty! Are you relying on a spouse, other family members, or friends to define you? If so, you need to recognize that their understanding of you is limited— and in some cases, they really don't know the real you at all! Are you relying on a boss, a teacher, or another person in a position of author- ity to define you? If so, that person neither knows you fully nor has the ability to see your past or your future.

God is the only reliable source of accurate, wise, eternal information about you. He alone loves you unconditionally, understands you fully, and knows the fullness of purpose that He has built into your life. If you are ever going to discover your *true* identity in Christ Jesus—if you are going to discover what it means to be a saint—you must turn to God and to His Word.

🔊 In what ways have you been relying upon others to give you a sense of self-worth or to define your identity?

"...whoever desires to become great among you, let him be your servant. And whoever desires to be first among you, let him be your slave—just as the Son of Man did not come to be served, but to serve, and to give His life a ransom for many."

—Matthew 20:26-28

❧ According to these verses, what were Jesus' purposes in coming to earth? How do these purposes relate to your identity?

❧ How do you react to the Lord's commandment to be a "slave"?

❧ Today and Tomorrow ❧

TODAY: A TOO-LOW SELF-ESTEEM LEADS TO THE SAME ERRORS AS A TOO-HIGH SELF-ESTEEM: I BECOME PROUD.

TOMORROW: I WILL ASK THE LORD TO SHOW ME THROUGH HIS WORD HOW TO HAVE A RIGHT SELF-ESTEEM.

LESSON 2

In Christ

─────────── ❧ **In This Lesson** ❧ ───────────

LEARNING: WHAT DOES IT MEAN TO BE "IN CHRIST"?

GROWING: HOW SHOULD MY IDENTITY IN CHRIST AFFECT MY VIEW OF MY-
SELF?

❧

Most Christians today do not seem to know who they are. If you ask people, "Who are you?" they are likely to respond with their name, where they work, whom they are related to, and so forth. One woman once said to me, "I'm Jane, wife of Tom, mother of Sally and Dennis, daughter of George and Ruth." She then went on to tell me the name of the company for which she worked. When I asked her, "But who are you as a Christian?" she stared at me blankly and finally said, "Well, I'm a member of *your church*!"

Many people give the name of a denomination or specific church for their identity as a Christian. Some believe that their identity as a Christian can be summed up by saying, "I'm baptized," "I'm a regular churchgoer," or "I've been saved for 22 years."

What you believe about yourself as a Christian determines your self-identity and your self-esteem. Our identity and esteem are not a matter of who we know, what kind of car we drive, where we work, which neighborhood we live in, or who our friends are. Our identity as believers flows from the relationship that we have with God through Christ Jesus, His Only begotten Son.

Who We are in Christ

It is critically important today that we know who we are in Christ. It is only when we know *who* we are that we can properly discern:

- how we are to respond in virtually any situation.

- how we are to make decisions in the face of virtually any problem or opportunity.

- how we are to answer virtually any question.

- how we are to treat other people.

- how we are to schedule our priorities in life.

- how we are to witness about Jesus Christ.

Our identity determines the way that we feel about ourselves, our hope for the future, and how we develop our talents and skills.

- Write a brief description below to answer this question: "Who are you?"

The apostle Paul was concerned about the true identity of the believer, and his foremost statement about the believer's identity can be summed up in two words: "in Christ." Notice the number of times that Paul uses the phrase "in Christ" in Ephesians 1:1–14:

> Paul, an apostle of Jesus Christ by the will of God, To the saints who are in Ephesus, and faithful in Christ Jesus:

> Grace to you and peace from God our Father and the Lord Jesus Christ.

> Blessed be the God and Father of our Lord Jesus Christ, who has blessed us with every spiritual blessing in the heavenly places in Christ, just as He chose us in Him before the foundation of the world, that we should be holy and without blame before Him in love, having predestined us to adoption as sons by Jesus Christ to Himself, according to the good pleasure of His will, to the praise of the glory of His grace, by which He made us accepted in the Beloved.

> In Him we have redemption through His blood, the forgiveness of sins, according to the riches of His grace which He made to abound toward us in all wisdom and prudence, having made known to us the mystery of His will, according to His good pleasure which He purposed in Himself, that in the dispensation of the fullness of the times He might gather together in one all things in Christ, both which are in heaven and which are on earth—in Him.

> In Him also we have obtained an inheritance, being predestined according to the purpose of Him who works all things according to the counsel of His will, that we who first trusted in Christ should be to the praise of His glory.

In Him you also trusted, after you heard the word of truth, the gospel of your salvation; in whom also, having believed, you were sealed with the Holy Spirit of promise, who is the guarantee of our inheritance until the redemption of the purchased possession, to the praise of His glory.

❧ In the passage above, circle the phrases "in Christ," "in Him," "in Himself," "in the Beloved" (who is Christ), and "in whom" (when it refers to Christ) whenever they appear.

❧ What exactly does it mean to be "in Christ"? How does your being "in Christ" change the very definition of who you are?

Our relationship with Christ is to be the inner motivation for our lives. It is to be our security and our confidence. Many people today are drawing their identity from the label in their dress or the name stitched onto their jeans, rather than drawing their identity from where their own name is written: in the Lamb's Book of Life! We are *in Christ*. If anyone asks you, "Who *are* you?" your answer should be this: "I am a believer in Christ Jesus. I am *in Christ*."

∽ Where Were You Before You Were in Christ? ∽

Where were you before you were in Christ? The Bible says that you were "in Adam." You were a natural heir of Adam, descended from the first man and woman created by God, who rebelled against God in their disobedience and who became subject to sin and spiritual death. You were born naturally with a sinful state of heart—your inclination was to sin, your desire was to sin. Nobody ever teaches a little child to steal, lie, or to covet toys. A child is born with a "me, myself, and I" complex. Paul describes this state of being "in Adam" in Ephesians 2:1–3:

> You He made alive, who were dead in trespasses and sins, in which you once walked according to the course of this world, according to the prince of the power of the air, the spirit who now works in the sons of disobedience, among whom also we all once conducted ourselves in the lusts of our flesh, fulfilling the desires of the flesh and of the mind, and were by nature children of wrath, just as the others.

In your sinful state, you had no way to bring about your own forgiveness or freedom from sin and guilt. No person can earn forgiveness. No person has the authority to say to himself, "You are forgiven."

A life "in Adam" is a life of darkness—blinded to the truth about God, separated from a relationship with God, and in bondage to sin's impulses—without genuine freedom to live a righteous life. It is a life headed for eternal death—the ultimate consequence of an unchanged sinful heart.

But God, who is rich in mercy, because of His great love with which He loved us, even when we were dead in trespasses, made us alive together with Christ (by grace you have been saved), and raised us up together, and made us sit together in the heavenly places in Christ Jesus.

—Ephesians 2:4-6

🔖 Note that these verses follow Ephesians 2:1-3, quoted above. What does it mean to be "dead in trespasses"?

🔖 If you were once dead, but have now been made alive again, what does this suggest about your identity "in Christ"?

∽ But Now, in Christ! ∽

Throughout his epistle, Paul gives a very vivid and complete description of our life "in Adam," but he does not end the story there. He goes on to give the hope and the great contrast of our life now as believers—a life *in Christ*. He wrote to the Ephesians, "But now in Christ Jesus you who once were far off have been brought near by the blood of Christ" (Ephesians 2:13).

The life that we have in Christ was made possible at God's initiative and at Christ Jesus' death on the cross. God was motivated by love to save mankind, and He did for man what man could not do for himself—He completely and eternally bridged the gap created by man's sin so that *all* who believe in Christ Jesus might be forgiven and have eternal life. John 3:16–18 tells us:

> For God so loved the world that He gave His only begotten Son, that whoever believes in Him should not perish but have everlasting life. For God did not send His Son into the world to condemn the world, but that the world through Him might be saved. He who believes in Him is not condemned; but he who does not believe is condemned already, because he has not believed in the name of the only begotten Son of God.

Believing and accepting the work that Jesus Christ did on the cross is *all* that is required for us to exchange our old identity "in Adam" to our new identity "in Christ." It is *all* that is required and, in fact, it is *the* requirement. No substitution for this requirement will work—no amount of good works, no amount of self-help techniques, no amount of thinking good thoughts or striving to be a good person. Paul made it very clear: "For by grace you have been saved through faith, and that not of yourselves; it is the gift of God, not of works, lest anyone should boast" (Ephesians 2:8–9).

> For since by man came death, by Man also came the resurrection of the dead. For as in Adam all die, even so in Christ all shall be made alive.
>
> —1 Corinthians 15:21-22

☙ Make a list of all the things that you inherited from Adam. In a parallel column, make a list of all that you inherited from Christ.

☙ Referring to the list in the last question, how would you define yourself when you were "in Adam"? How would you define yourself now "in Christ"?

Our Life in Christ

Throughout the New Testament, we find a number of descriptions about what it means to be made alive "in Christ." Paul writes in 2 Corinthians 5:17–18:

> Therefore, if anyone is in Christ, he is a new creation; old things have passed away; behold, all things have become new. Now all things are of God, who has reconciled us to Himself through Jesus Christ.

19

Once we are in Christ, we are not to draw from a deposit of previous good works; we are not to believe the "old lies" that have been playing in our heads since early childhood that we are worthless, unwanted, or undesirable. We are new creatures with a new life ahead—a life that is totally reconciled to God and is set on a path toward fulfillment and satisfaction in Christ Jesus.

John described our life in Christ as a branch abiding in a vine. He recorded these words of Jesus (John 15:5–8):

> I am the vine, you are the branches. He who abides in Me, and
> I in him, bears much fruit; for without Me you can do nothing.
> If anyone does not abide in Me, he is cast out as a branch and
> is withered; and they gather them and throw them into the fire,
> and they are burned. If you abide in Me, and My words abide
> in you, you will ask what you desire, and it shall be done for
> you. By this My Father is glorified, that you bear much fruit; so
> you will be My disciples.

🙠 In what ways does a branch depend upon the trunk for survival and nourishment? Give practical ways in which you are called to do the same in Christ.

🙠 What does it mean to "abide in" Christ? Give practical examples of how this is done.

The person who is in Christ will have a heart bent toward God. He will be able to receive and enjoy those things that the Lord has reserved exclusively for believers. He will be empowered to live a godly life. He will pursue a life that is marked by the fruit of the Holy Spirit and by a bold witness for Christ Jesus.

What freedom this gives us! We are not destined to receive what we deserved when we were "in Adam"—rather, we are destined to receive what God loves to give us "in Christ"! No more striving, no more climbing the ladder of acceptability, no more performing in hopes of gaining God's applause. Our new life in Christ is not based upon what we do, but on who we *are* in Christ.

> Therefore, if anyone is in Christ, he is a new creation; old things have passed away; behold, all things have become new.
>
> —2 Corinthians 5:17

What "old things" have passed away from your identity before becoming a Christian? What things have "become new" in your identity?

Write below a brief statement of who you are "in Christ". How does this statement compare with the one that you wrote at the beginning of this lesson?

Today and Tomorrow

TODAY: MY TRUE IDENTITY COMES ENTIRELY THROUGH THE GRACE AND SACRIFICE OF JESUS CHRIST.

TOMORROW: I WILL PRAYERFULLY STUDY THE SCRIPTURES THIS WEEK TO LEARN WHAT IT MEANS TO BE "IN CHRIST".

Notes and Prayer Requests:

LESSON 3

Chosen by God

☙ In This Lesson ❧

LEARNING: WHAT DOES IT MEAN TO BE "CHOSEN BY GOD"?

GROWING: IF I HAVE BEEN ADOPTED BY GOD, HOW SHOULD THAT AFFECT MY LIFE?

Are you aware that, as a believer in Christ Jesus, you have been chosen by God? What a wonderful word that is! *Chosen* automatically speaks to us of value, worthiness, love, and appreciation. To be chosen means that others *want* to be with us, *want* to know us, *want* to spend time with us. Certainly all of those things are true when it comes to God's choosing to be reconciled to us in Christ Jesus and choosing us as His children. In choosing us, God is saying, "I want to be in a close relationship with you; I want to spend time with you; I want to share Myself with you."

As a believer in Christ Jesus, you are a saint in Christ, *and* you have been chosen by God to have a very special relationship with Him.

The apostle Paul wrote in Ephesians 1:3–4:

Blessed be the God and Father of our Lord Jesus Christ, who has blessed us with every spiritual blessing in the heavenly places in Christ, just as *He chose us in Him before the foundation of the world*, that we should be holy and without blame before Him in love. (*emphasis added*)

᠃ When have you felt "chosen" for something special? How did you respond to being "chosen"?

᠃ What does it mean to you to know that you have been personally chosen by God?

God Does the Choosing

As we study what it means to be chosen by God, we must be very certain about one thing: it is God who does the choosing. Paul wrote that "He chose us in Him before the foundation of the world" (Ephesians 1:4). In other words, from the very beginning of all things, God *planned* to be in relationship with you through Christ Jesus. You were always a part of God's plan and purpose, you were always chosen by God—even before you personally accepted Jesus as your Savior. You have always been a *desired* child of God.

So many children grow up being told by their parents, "We never really wanted you. You were an accident. You were a 'surprise.'" The truth from God's perspective is something entirely different: God *always* wanted you. You were part of His design and His plan from the foundation of the earth. You were intended, expected, and created by God for precisely this time and for a precise purpose. God didn't say when you were born, "Well, what can I do about this child?" No! God said at your birth, "This is the child whom I created for this specific time, place, and purpose on the earth!" Furthermore, Paul wrote that God chose us "according to the good pleasure of His will" (Ephesians 1:5). In other words, God created you because it *pleased* Him to create you.

None of us can ever fathom God's grace in choosing us. Nothing that you ever did or could do put you into a position to be chosen by God. You didn't say the right things, do the right things, or become the right person. God chose you because He *wanted* to choose you and because He desired to be in relationship with you. He made a sovereign choice, totally from His own motivation of love and mercy.

"Grace" is the undeserved favor of God at work in our lives, and we are the recipients of divine grace. Our being chosen is the act of a loving God, who chose us solely because He gained pleasure in doing so.

But you are a chosen generation, a royal priesthood, a holy nation, His own special people, that you may proclaim the praises of Him who called you out of darkness into His marvelous light.

—1 Peter 2:9

❧ Put into your own words what each of the following means. Give practical examples.

Chosen generation:

Royal priesthood:

Holy nation:

Special people:

❧ For what purpose has God chosen you, according to this verse? How does this purpose influence your perspective about yourself?

Predestined to Be Adopted

In Ephesians 1:4–5, Paul conveyed this truth of our being "chosen" by using two very specific terms: *predestined* and *adopted*. He says about God the Father,

> He chose us in Him [Christ] before the foundation of the world
> ... having *predestined* us to *adoption* as sons by Jesus Christ to
> Himself. (*emphasis added*)

Does God make choices? Yes! God *chose* Israel: "...My people, My chosen. This people I have formed for Myself; They shall declare My praise" (Isaiah 43:20–21). God *chose* Jesus to be the Lamb slain from the foundation of the world (Revelation 13:8). God *chose* you to be His person on the earth today.

Many Christians are divided on the issue of predestination. There are those who advocate "whosoever will," and they put the emphasis on man's choice to receive God's love and forgiveness. There are those who advocate "predestined," and they put the emphasis on God's will to choose man by pouring out His love and forgiveness as He desires. The fact is—both are correct! The invitation to receive God's forgiveness is extended to all, and the net result is that some are chosen.

Paul spoke clearly to the Ephesians about being predestined, but he also had this to say about the Hebrew people, who saw themselves as the chosen people of God:

> I could wish that I myself were accursed from Christ for my
> brethren, my countrymen according to the flesh, who are Isra-
> elites, to whom pertain the adoption, the glory, the covenants,
> the giving of the law, the service of God, and the promises; of
> whom are the fathers and from whom, according to the flesh,
> Christ came, who is over all, the eternally blessed God. Amen.

But it is not that the word of God has taken no effect. For they are not all Israel who are of Israel, nor are they all children because they are the seed of Abraham ... Why? Because they did not seek it by faith, but as it were, by the works of the law ... Brethren, my heart's desire and prayer to God for Israel is that they may be saved.

—Romans 9:3–7, 32; 10:1

Paul was the first to say that not all of Israel, the "chosen people," were predestined to salvation. He concluded, "Whoever calls on the name of the LORD shall be saved" (Romans 10:13). Paul invested his life in preaching the gospel to *all* with whom he had contact. He writes in Corinthians 9:19–23:

For though I am free from all men, I have made myself a servant to all, that I might win the more; and to the Jews I became as a Jew, that I might win Jews; to those who are under the law, as under the law, that I might win those who are under the law; to those who are without law, as without law (not being without law toward God, but under law toward Christ), that I might win those who are without law; to the weak I became as weak, that I might win the weak. *I have become all things to all men, that I might by all means save some. Now this I do for the gospel's sake, that I may be partaker of it with you.* (*emphasis added*)

No person can ever fully understand this matter of man's free will and God's predestined choice. It is a matter of faith—accepting God's Word as truth and recognizing that we have been *chosen* by God to be saints in Christ. Prior to our salvation and our acceptance of Christ, each of us fell into the "whosoever will" category (see John 3:16). After we accept Christ, we find ourselves in the "predestined" category.

🕊 Can you recall experiences in which the Lord seemed to be wooing you to receive Jesus?

The Lord is not slack concerning His promise, as some count slackness, but is longsuffering toward us, not willing that any should perish but that all should come to repentance.

—2 Peter 3:9

"For many are called, but few are chosen."

—Matthew 22:14

🕊 How do you reconcile these two verses? How can you be both "called" and "chosen"?

Do not focus on what might have been if you had not received God's forgiveness and accepted Jesus Christ as your Savior; instead, put your focus on who you are as a believer. You are a chosen saint of God, chosen from the foundation of the world.

Our Adoption

Paul further wrote that we were predestined for a very specific role: to be an adopted child of God (see Ephesians 1:5). Adoption in Paul's day was a little different than it is today. A father in Rome might disown a natural-born child, but a father could not legally disown an adopted child. Adopted children had full rights to all that a father might leave as an inheritance and to the full use of the father's name. Adoption was highly prized in Rome because it carried with it great legal privileges and societal recognition. In a culture in which natural-born children were often overlooked, discarded, or shut out of a father's presence, adopted children were conveyed the full rights of "sonship."

Paul's goal in writing to the Ephesians was that they understand their position in Christ—God had chosen them to be *sons*. They were in a privileged position before God!

> But when the fullness of the time had come, God sent forth His Son, born of a woman, born under the law, to redeem those who were under the law, that we might receive the adoption as sons.... Therefore you are no longer a slave but a son, and if a son, then an heir of God through Christ.
>
> —Galatians 4:4-5, 7

List some of the differences between being a "slave" and being a "son".

๛ How do these things change your view of yourself before God?

Not a Cause for Boasting

You are a chosen saint of God, predestined from the foundation of the world as an adopted child of God. What an awesome identity you have as a believer in Christ! But is this cause for boasting? Is our identity a reason to separate ourselves from other people or to think of ourselves more highly than those who are still "in Adam"? No!

Rather than a cause for boasting, our identity in Christ as a chosen, adopted child should give us more compassion for those who are outside Christ. We should be more compelled to share the gospel so that others might be among the "whosoever will." Knowing the great privilege it is to be a chosen child of God, we should seek to bring others into fellowship with us, so that they, too, might be joint heirs with Christ of all things and the recipient of all spiritual blessings!

God hates pride wherever He finds it (see Proverbs 16:18). Pride will have no place in heaven. We are wise to come humbly before God with praise and thanksgiving for choosing us, and say to Him, "Abba, Father, thank You for choosing me to be Your child."

It is as we recognize that we are chosen that we then must choose to serve, choose to witness, and choose to praise God with every breath that we take.

For as many as are led by the Spirit of God, these are sons of God. For you did not receive the spirit of bondage again to fear, but you received the Spirit of adoption by whom we cry out, "Abba, Father."

—Romans 8:14-15

❧ ⬧Abba" means "daddy" in Hebrew. Have you ever called God "Daddy" when praying? How does that intimacy affect your view of yourself?

❧ What is the "spirit of bondage to fear"? How does fear influence your view of yourself? How does your adoption by God influence that fear?

❧ Today and Tomorrow ❧

TODAY: I HAVE BEEN BOTH CALLED AND CHOSEN BY GOD HIMSELF—AND THAT ALONE MAKES ME VALUABLE.

TOMORROW: I WILL SPEND TIME IN WORSHIP AND THANKSGIVING THIS WEEK, PRAISING GOD FOR ADOPTING ME.

❧ Notes and Prayer Requests: ❧

Lesson 4

Beloved Child

◈ In This Lesson ◈

Learning: Why does God love me?

Growing: How does God's love influence my identity?

You are not only God's adopted child, but you are God's beloved child. His love for you is unconditional and unlimited! Many people have a difficult time accepting the love of God. Others accept God's love, but place conditions on it. It is important that we acknowledge God's unconditional love as part of our spiritual identity, because the degree to which we receive unconditional love is directly linked to the degree that we are able to give unconditional love to others.

Do you put qualifiers on God's love? Do you find yourself "objecting" to the fact that God loves you? If so, you are rejecting a part of your spiritual identity as a believer—the fact that you *are* the beloved child of God.

◈ How do you feel when you hear the words, "God loves you"?

❧ What do you feel you need to do in order to be loved by God? What areas of your life are dictated by a need to earn His love?

Love Is Our Status in Christ

Paul wrote in Ephesians 1:6 that the believer is "accepted in the Beloved". The "Beloved," of course, is Christ Jesus. Few would argue that God the Father loved Jesus Christ, His Only begotten Son. It is inconceivable to think that a loving God would not love the Son, a member of the holy Trinity!

As believers, we are "in Christ." Our entire identity before God the Father is clothed in the righteousness and identity of Jesus Christ. We are part of the Beloved—we are loved because we are in Christ Jesus and God loves Jesus.

In this the love of God was manifested toward us, that God has sent His only begotten Son into the world, that we might live through Him. In this is love, not that we loved God, but that He loved us and sent His Son to be the propitiation for our sins.

—1 John 4:9-10

∞ According to these verses, how much does God love you? Why does He love you?

∞ According to these verses, what have you done to win God's love? What can you do in the future to retain His love?

The Characteristics of God's Love

God's love pours from His infinite and eternal heart, at God's will. God *chooses* to love. He initiates love. He does not "react" to love; He loves *first*. As John wrote, "We love Him because He first loved us" (1 John 4:19). Read what Paul wrote in Titus 3:4–6 about God's love initiative:

But when the kindness and the love of God our Savior toward man appeared, not by works of righteousness which we have done, but according to His mercy He saved us, through the washing of regeneration and renewing of the Holy Spirit, whom He poured out on us abundantly through Jesus Christ our Savior.

We didn't earn the coming of Jesus Christ. We didn't "deserve" the death of God's Son on the cross. We didn't qualify ourselves to be recipients of God's kindness, love, or mercy. God *chose* to love us, and He continues to choose to love us.

When have you loved another person unconditionally, even though that person may not have seemed "worthy" of love? Who has done that for you?

Who has given freely and "abundantly" to you in your life? How does God's abundance of the Holy Spirit influence your views of yourself?

∞ God's Love Is Everlasting ∞

The Lord spoke these words through the prophet Jeremiah (Jeremiah 31:3):

> Yes, I have loved you with an everlasting love; Therefore with lovingkindness I have drawn you.

The good news about God's love is that there is nothing that you can do to make God "un-love" you. So many Christians seem to think that, when they sin or fall short of God's plan for their lives, they disappoint God and He ceases to love them—at least temporarily. No! The fact is, there is nothing you have ever done to deserve God's love. No amount of good works, kindness, perfected personality, or charitable deeds can win God's love. God chooses to love, and the motivation rests entirely in Him. He loves because He is loving. As John wrote, "God is love" (1 John 4:8). It is God's nature to love, and His nature does not change according to human behavior. There is nothing that you have done or ever could do to earn God's love, and there is nothing that you can ever do to stop God from loving you, not even for a moment. His love for you is *everlasting*.

> For God so loved the world that He gave His only begotten Son, that whoever believes in Him should not perish but have everlasting life.
>
> —John 3:16

∞ According to this verse, what did you do to gain eternal life? What did God do?

✎ What does this suggest regarding God's love for you personally? What does it suggest about your true identity?

∽ God Loves What God Creates ∽

When God created you, He loved you. Stated another way, God does not create what God does not love. Everything that God created was declared to be "good"—perfect, whole, valuable, lovable. God doesn't make junk. He doesn't make messes. God creates what He considers to be worthy of His love, His tender care, and His eternal presence.

Furthermore, God does not pour out His Spirit on what God does not love. When you accepted Jesus Christ as your Savior, God immediately moved into your life by the power of the Holy Spirit. God does not reside in a vessel that He does not love.

Paul writes in Ephesians 2:8–9: "For by grace you have been saved through faith, and that not of yourselves; it is the gift of God, not of works, lest anyone should boast." God is in the process of making you and fulfilling you and bringing you to the full purpose of your life. He is transforming you into the likeness of Jesus Christ. And He is doing so with tender and infinite love for you. God is fashioning you and molding you and chiseling you to be the beloved child with whom He desires to live forever.

God loves what God makes—including *you!*

Now hope does not disappoint, because the love of God has been poured out in our hearts by the Holy Spirit who was given to us.

—Romans 5:5

✎ What does it mean that "hope does not disappoint"? Give examples from your own life where hope encouraged you or kept you going.

✎ In what ways does the Holy Spirit bring us hope? How does the Holy Spirit's presence in your life affect your identity in the eyes of God?

∽ Nothing Can Separate You from God's Love ∽

You cannot cause God to stop loving you, and nothing else can keep God from loving you. As a believer in Christ Jesus, no outside force can cause God to stop loving you or separate you from His love. Paul was very clear in Romans 8:35–39:

Who shall separate us from the love of Christ? Shall tribulation, or distress, or persecution, or famine, or nakedness, or peril, or sword? As it is written:

"For Your sake we are killed all day long; We are accounted as sheep for the slaughter."

Yet in all these things we are more than conquerors through Him *who loved us*. For I am persuaded that neither death nor life, nor angels nor principalities nor powers, nor things present nor things to come, nor height nor depth, nor any other created thing, shall be able to separate us from the love of God which is in Christ Jesus our Lord. (*emphasis added*)

꙳ List below everything that you've ever thought could make God stop loving you. Then go through Paul's list of things that *cannot* separate you from His love (in the verses above), and cross out anything in *your* list that is included in *Paul's* list.

Our Response to God's Love

We are to have three responses to God's love for us.

1. Accept God's Love

First, we are to acknowledge God's love and accept it. My prayer for you is the prayer of Paul for the Thessalonians: "Now may the Lord direct your hearts into the love of God" (2 Thessalonians 3:5). Receive God's love. Open your heart to God as you pray, "Lord, I know that You love me according to the truth of Your Word. Help me to receive Your love fully so that I feel Your loving presence always."

2. Live in God's Love

God's love is part of God's nature—His love is *always* flowing toward us. In Jude 21 we read, "Keep yourselves in the love of God, looking for the mercy of our Lord Jesus Christ unto eternal life." 1 John 4:16 also tells us that "God is love, and he who abides in love abides in God, and God in him."

As believers in Christ Jesus, we are to nurture our understanding of God's love and seek to dwell in His love daily. Thank the Lord each morning for His love. Remind yourself often, "God loves me!"

3. Love Others

As we fully receive and abide in God's love, we are to be vessels for His love, poured out to others. Loving others is not just a nice idea; it is a commandment of God. Jesus said,

This is My commandment, that you love one another as I have loved you. Greater love has no one than this, than to lay down one's life for his friends.

—John 15:12–13

👁 How has Jesus loved you? Give specific examples, both from Scripture and from your own life.

👁 According to these verses, how are you called to love others? How does this calling affect your identity?

Experiencing More of God's Love

Those who abide in God's love and seek to express God's love to others will experience even *more* of God's love in their lives. This does not mean that God loves them more; God's love is infinite and eternal at all times. Rather, it means that those who abide in love and who are expressing love *experience* God's love in their own lives in increasingly profound and joyful ways. Paul writes in Ephesians 3:14, 17–19:

I bow my knees to the Father of our Lord Jesus Christ ... that Christ may dwell in your hearts through faith; that you, being rooted and grounded in love, may be able to comprehend with all the saints what is the width and length and depth and height—to know the love of Christ which passes knowledge; that you may be filled with all the fullness of God.

If you desire to *feel* more of God's love and to grow in your relationship with God, receive God's love by faith, choose to abide in God's love daily, and show God's love to others. What you give of God's love will be what you receive back—in multiplied form!

If someone says, "I love God," and hates his brother, he is a liar; for he who does not love his brother whom he has seen, how can he love God whom he has not seen? And this commandment we have from Him: that he who loves God must love his brother also.

—1 John 4:20-21

☙ How do these verses compare with the world's teaching that we are supposed to love ourselves? Why does John command us to love others, rather than telling us to love ourselves?

☙ List below one or two people that you have trouble loving. What will you do this week to show them God's love?

Finally, all of you be of one mind, having compassion for one another; love as brothers, be tenderhearted, be courteous; not returning evil for evil or reviling for reviling, but on the contrary blessing, knowing that you were called to this, that you may inherit a blessing.

—1 Peter 3:8-9

Give specific examples of each of the following:

Having compassion:

Loving as brothers:

Be tenderhearted:

Be courteous:

Blessing for evil:

Blessing for reviling:

❧ Today and Tomorrow ❧

TODAY: NOTHING CAN EVER SEPARATE ME FROM GOD'S LOVE—NOTHING IN HEAVEN, EARTH, OR HELL!

TOMORROW: I WILL MAKE A DELIBERATE EFFORT TO SHOW GOD'S LOVE TO OTHERS, LOVING THEM AS I LOVE MYSELF.

❧ Notes and Prayer Requests: ❧

LESSON 5

Redeemed

❧ In This Lesson ❧

LEARNING: WHAT DIFFERENCE DOES IT MAKE THAT MY SINS ARE FORGIVEN?

GROWING: HOW DOES MY SALVATION AFFECT MY IDENTITY?

Are you living today knowing fully that you are redeemed? Do you have the identity of a person who has been freed of sin's bondage? Do you feel fully and forever forgiven?

Many Christians today *say* that they have been forgiven of all their sins, but they often say this with a small question mark in their voices—they are *hoping* that they are forgiven fully rather than *knowing with certainty* that they are forgiven. Others believe that their sins have been forgiven, but they continue to struggle with sin, and they wonder if their ongoing struggle means that they were not fully forgiven—they have questions about whether they can ever be free of sinful desires and old sinful habits.

Paul wrote this wonderful statement about our identity as believers in Ephesians 1:7:

In Him we have redemption through His blood, the forgiveness of sins, according to the riches of His grace.

In this lesson, we will deal with our true identity as those who have been "redeemed by the blood of Christ Jesus."

⮞ When have you wondered whether God had truly forgiven you of your sin nature? When have you struggled with an ongoing desire to sin?

⮞ According to Ephesians 1:7, how can you know that God has fully forgiven you? What does His forgiveness depend on?

Forgiveness of Our Sins

Paul uses two words to describe the believer's relationship to sin: *redemption* and *forgiveness*. We'll deal with the second of these terms first, since it is the term with which most of us are more familiar.

To be forgiven is to be set free from any guilt over past sins. It is to have the "sin slate" totally wiped clean. Sin is regarded throughout the Bible as a state of bondage resulting from transgressions and evil. We commit sin because we *are* sinners. We were born with a sin nature. Our sinful actions further seal the fact that we are sinners.

Every sinner knows that he is sinning. Sin involves the will, and it involves our memory. We remember our sins. They don't just float by unnoticed or ignored. The psalmist acknowledged this in Psalm 51:3: "For I acknowledge my transgressions, And my sin is always before me." Each of us is born with a sin nature and each of us commits sin. Therefore, each of us is in need of forgiveness. There is no person who is naturally good or without sin. Every person is in need of God's salvation so that we do not experience the spiritual consequences of sin.

> For all have sinned and fall short of the glory of God.

> —Romans 3:23

∾ What does it mean to "fall short of the glory of God"? What *is* "the glory of God"? How far short have you fallen?

∾ What part does sin play in your self-identity?

49

Before:

Our state prior to receiving God's forgiveness is this: *we were living in sin, the end result of which is eternal death*. God's nature is holiness and truth, and He cannot abide where evil and unrighteousness are allowed to reign. God loves the sinner always, but He is never content to allow a sinner to continue in sin because, as long as the person continues in sin, he is just beyond the reach of God's forgiveness. God is always working to bring a sinner to the forgiveness offered through Jesus Christ so that He might cause a spiritual rebirth in that person and abide with him.

After:

Our state *after* receiving God's forgiveness is this: *we are living in the righteousness of Jesus Christ, and we inherit eternal life*. By the power of His Holy Spirit, God abides within us and lives His life through us.

Every believer is a walking picture of "before and after." Before Christ, we were unforgiven and were on a path to eternal death. In Christ, we are forgiven and are on a path toward eternal life.

> And you He made alive, who were dead in trespasses and sins.
>
> —Ephesians 2:1

⁊ How can a dead person become alive again? According to this verse, how did *you* become alive again? How does this influence your identity?

Likewise you also, reckon yourselves to be dead indeed to sin, but alive to God in Christ Jesus our Lord.

—Romans 6:11

How does a dead person respond to temptation? How can such a "reckoning" help you strengthen your self-identity?

Total Forgiveness

Many people think that their slate of sins has been only partially wiped clean. They look at the seriousness of their sin and wonder, "Could God ever fully forgive *that type of sin*?" Others look at the great number of their sins and question, "Could God ever fully forgive *so much sin*?" Still others look at the magnitude of a particular sin and ask, "Could God ever fully forgive *such a great sin*?" The answer to each question is an unqualified yes!

In the first place, God does not place qualifiers on sin. No one type of sin is any greater or lesser, blacker or darker, than any other kind of sin. Before God, sin is sin. Neither does God look at the amount of sin in a person's life and declare that, with the addition of one more sin, a person moves from a "forgivable" to an "unforgivable" column. All sin, no matter the amount, is equal before God—one sin is the same as one million sins, one type of sin is just as serious as any other.

When God forgives sin, He forgives it completely, even to the point of *forgetting it entirely*! Not one shred of sin is left over for later forgiveness. God's ability to forgive sin is infinite and inexhaustible.

> ...But You have lovingly delivered my soul from the pit of corruption, For You have cast all my sins behind Your back.
>
> —Isaiah 38:17

☙ According to this verse, which of your sins has God "cast behind His back"?

> As far as the east is from the west, So far has He removed our transgressions from us.
>
> —Psalm 103:12

☙ How far is the east from the west? If you travel around the globe heading east, at what point will you begin heading west?

☙ What does this imply about God's forgiveness of *your* sins?

∞ No One Who Seeks God's Forgiveness is Turned Away ∞

One awe-inspiring aspect of God's character is that He is merciful and forgiving to all who seek His forgiveness. All who ask God for forgiveness are granted it. Jesus said, "The one who comes to Me I will by no means cast out" (John 6:37). Our part is to come to God with a humble heart and to confess that we have sinned and are in need of forgiveness, to accept Jesus Christ's sacrifice on the cross, and to receive the forgiveness that God offers. God's response to our confession is always to forgive.

There simply is no basis for *not* accepting God's forgiveness—it is freely offered to all; it costs us nothing to receive; and it results in the guaranteed benefits of freedom from guilt and eternal life!

∞ Have you confessed your sins and received God's forgiveness? If not, what is preventing you from doing so right now?

Repent therefore and be converted, that your sins may be blotted out, so that times of refreshing may come from the presence of the Lord.

—Acts 3:19

❧ What does it mean to have your "sins blotted out"? If ink is erased, how can it be "un-erased"?

❧ How does this fact influence your identity?

∞ Our Lingering Guilt ∞

Many people experience God's forgiveness but then suffer from lingering guilt over their past sins. If we hang on to guilt after receiving God's forgiveness, we are saying to God, "Your forgiveness wasn't enough." And surely it is! The challenge for many of us is to *accept* God's total forgiveness and then to forgive ourselves and move forward in our lives. To hang on to guilt and shame is to devalue what Christ Jesus did on the cross.

What areas of guilt from past sin do you still hold on to? What past sins do you still "beat yourself up" over?

> Jesus answered them, "Most assuredly, I say to you, whoever commits sin is a slave of sin. And a slave does not abide in the house forever, but a son abides forever. Therefore if the Son makes you free, you shall be free indeed."

> —John 8:34-36

What power transforms a person from being a "slave" to being a "son"? According to this verse, what power can turn a son back into a slave?

How does this permanent freedom affect your identity?

Redeemed from Being a Slave to Sin

Not only are you forgiven, but you have been redeemed from sin's bondage. To be redeemed is to be "delivered by payment of debt." Redemption is the *purchase* of something that has a debt against it. We see this in the way that pawnshops are operated: those who buy things at pawnshops are buying items that have a debt against them. As we discussed earlier in this lesson, sinners carry a "debt" of sin. In their sinful state, they are living under a death sentence.

When Christ died on the cross, He paid our sin debt and purchased us for God. Paul compared our purchase to the slave markets of the Roman Empire. He writes in Romans 6:16–18, 22:

> Do you not know that to whom you present yourselves slaves
> to obey, you are that one's slaves whom you obey, whether of
> sin leading to death, or of obedience leading to righteousness?
> But God be thanked that though you were slaves of sin, yet
> you obeyed from the heart ... And having been set free from
> sin, you became slaves of righteousness ... Now having been
> set free from sin, and having become slaves of God, you have
> your fruit to holiness, and the end, everlasting life.

Slaves do what they are compelled to do by their masters. Paul stated that those who are still in a sinful state are slaves to their sin nature. They behave as they do because their sin nature compels them to do what is unrighteous in God's eyes. Those who have received God's forgiveness, however, have the Holy Spirit dwelling within them, and they are compelled to act in a righteous way because of His presence.

～ When have you felt compelled to sin even though you knew that it was wrong before God?

Only a free person can buy a slave, and the only truly "free" person who ever walked this earth was Christ Jesus. He was the only One capable of purchasing us from the "slave market of sin." By His shed blood, He made it possible for us to be forgiven and redeemed *so that we no longer have a sin nature and we no longer are slaves to sin.*

This means that we as believers in Christ Jesus do not *have* to sin. The Holy Spirit dwelling in us will do His utmost to keep us from sinning, and if we sin, the Holy Spirit will convict us so that we will confess our sin and repent of it. To sin is no longer our natural impulse. Sin has become unnatural and abhorrent to us. Our redemption means that we are now in the process of losing all desire to sin. John tells us in 1 John 2:1, 3–6:

> If anyone sins, we have an Advocate with the Father, Jesus Christ the righteous ... Now by this we know that we know Him, if we keep His commandments. He who says, "I know Him," and does not keep His commandments, is a liar, and the truth is not in him. But whoever keeps His word, truly the love of God is perfected in him. By this we know that we are in Him. He who says he abides in Him ought himself also to walk just as He walked.

~ Even though a son cannot be forced back into slavery, he might still choose to *act* like a slave. When has this been true in your own life?

~ What does Jesus say about His children acting like slaves? Why does He take this issue so seriously?

∞ Can We Really Live Any Way That We Want? ∞

Many people question the security of salvation, falsely believing that a Christian can be saved and then live any way that he chooses without consequence. There is always consequence to sin! The believer in Christ Jesus will not lose his salvation and eternal life if he chooses to sin, but he is setting himself up for a lifetime of misery if he sins in the face of God's loving forgiveness. The Holy Spirit acts within the believer to convict him of sin and to draw him immediately back to the throne of God, to confess that sin and to receive forgiveness for it. The person who pursues a life of sin has probably not been born again. As John writes in 1 John 5:1–4:

Whoever believes that Jesus is the Christ is born of God, and everyone who loves Him who begot also loves him who is begotten of Him. By this we know that we love the children of God, when we love God and keep His commandments. For this is the love of God, that we keep His commandments. And His commandments are not burdensome. For whatever is born of God overcomes the world. And this is the victory that has overcome the world—our faith.

The person who has been redeemed and forgiven of his sins will no longer have a desire or an automatic impulse to sin. Rather, the very *nature* of the person has been changed so that his desire is for the things of God.

What shall we say then? Shall we continue in sin that grace may abound? Certainly not! How shall we who died to sin live any longer in it?

—Romans 6:1-2

ᕛ When have you chosen to sin, telling yourself, "It's ok—God will forgive me"?

ᕛ If you died in a car crash, you would never drive again. How does this apply to your attitude toward temptation? How does being "dead to sin" affect your identity?

Living with a Forgiven Identity

Those who have been forgiven are called to do three things: to forgive others, to share God's message of forgiveness with others, and to walk as forgiven saints in Christ Jesus.

To forgive others is a commandment. Jesus said,

> ❧ "Be merciful, just as your Father also is merciful. Judge not, and you shall not be judged. Condemn not, and you shall not be condemned. Forgive, and you will be forgiven." (Luke 6:36–37)

> ❧ "And whenever you stand praying, if you have anything against anyone, forgive him, that your Father in heaven may also forgive you your trespasses. But if you do not forgive, neither will your Father in heaven forgive your trespasses." (Mark 11:25–26)

> ❧ "Then his master, after he had called him, said to him, 'You wicked servant! I forgave you all that debt because you begged me. Should you not also have had compassion on your fellow servant, just as I had pity on you?' And his master was angry, and delivered him to the torturers until he should pay all that was due to him. So My heavenly Father also will do to you if each of you, from his heart, does not forgive his brother his trespasses." (Matthew 18:32–35)

We have received forgiveness freely from the Lord, and we are to freely give it to others (see Matthew 10:8).

✎ Why is it vitally important that we forgive others, according to these verses?

✎ According to Mark 11:25-26 above, when should we forgive others? How often? For what?

∽ Proclaiming God's Forgiveness ∽

We are never to keep the good news of God's forgiveness to ourselves—we are to use every opportunity to tell others about God's love and salvation. In forgiving others, we give witness to God's desire to forgive. But we must go beyond the example of our lives to actually telling others that God loves them and *how* they can receive God's forgiveness.

> And He said to them, "Go into all the world and preach the gospel to every creature."
>
> —Mark 16:15

✎ Where does Jesus command us to preach? To whom are we commanded to preach the gospel?

∽ Living in Repentance ∽

Finally, we are to live as forgiven saints, walking boldly into the life that God has for us. This means true repentance—turning from all things that we know are displeasing to God and choosing to obey His commandments. Our identity is no longer associated with darkness, evil, guilt, shame, or death. Rather, our identity is linked to light, goodness, love, joy, and eternal life. We are to walk truly as children of the light!

If we say that we have fellowship with Him, and walk in darkness, we lie and do not practice the truth. But if we walk in the light as He is in the light, we have fellowship with one another, and the blood of Jesus Christ His Son cleanses us from all sin.

—1 John 1:6-7

∾ What does it mean to "walk in darkness"? Give examples from your own life of times when you chose to walk in darkness.

∾ What does it mean to "practice the truth"? Why does truth need "practice"? How does this affect your identity in Christ?

∾ **Today and Tomorrow** ∾

TODAY: JESUS REDEEMED ME FROM SLAVERY TO SIN, MAKING ME A SON OF GOD!

TOMORROW: I WILL REMEMBER THAT A SON OF GOD SHOULD NOT ACT LIKE A SLAVE TO SIN.

∽ Notes and Prayer Requests: ∽

LESSON 6

Heir

--- ❧ **In This Lesson** ❧ ---

LEARNING: WHAT DOES IT MEAN TO BE AN HEIR TOGETHER WITH CHRIST?

GROWING: WHAT EXACTLY IS MY INHERITANCE, AND WHAT DIFFERENCE DOES IT MAKE NOW?

✷

Are you aware that you are the recipient of a grand inheritance? Many people daydream of receiving an unexpected inheritance from a wealthy person. The fact is, as a believer in Christ Jesus, you *are* the heir of the most lavish inheritance that any person could ever dream to receive!

Paul writes in Ephesians 1:11, "In Him also we have obtained an inheritance." And what is that inheritance? Paul describes it in these terms in Ephesians and elsewhere:

❧ "blessed us with every spiritual blessing in the heavenly places in Christ" (Ephesians 1:3)

❧ "exceeding riches of His grace" (Ephesians 2:7)

❧ "treasure in earthen vessels" (2 Corinthians 4:7)

❧ "riches of His glory" (Ephesians 3:16)

Paul declared, "Eye has not seen, nor ear heard, Nor have entered into the heart of man The things which God has prepared for those who love Him" (1 Corinthians 2:9). The inheritance that we have in Christ Jesus is so glorious, so vast, and so tremendous that we cannot even comprehend it with our finite minds. Paul writes in Ephesians 3:20–21, "Now to Him who is able to do *exceedingly abundantly above all that we ask or think,* according to the power that works in us, to Him be glory in the church by Christ Jesus to all generations, forever and ever. Amen" (*emphasis added*). The inheritance that God has prepared for us is an overflowing, abundant inheritance. Nothing of benefit or goodness has been withheld from us.

☙ What is the most impossible thing that you've ever prayed for? What is the most wonderful miracle that you've ever day-dreamed about?

☙ Whatever miracles you listed above, note that God is able to do—not just those miracles—but "exceedingly abundantly above all that we ask or think." What does this suggest about your inheritance in Christ?

Rich or Poor?

Many Christians see themselves as being poor. Some have this identity because they have been taught incorrectly that Christians are to be poor and uneducated. There is no justification in Scripture for a Christian to be either poor or ignorant. To the contrary, Paul declares in Philippians 4:19, "My God shall supply all your need according to His riches in glory by Christ Jesus." We are to study and know the truth of God's Word and to be well-informed about our inheritance.

Rich or poor is never a matter of one's bank account. Richness and poverty are states of the heart—we respond to life with generosity or stinginess, with fear or boldness, based on how rich we believe ourselves to be in Christ Jesus and how much we are trusting God to supply all of our needs. Our identity as believers must always be based upon what we know to be true in God's Word, not on how we feel or what others say about us. We must never draw our identity from unbelievers. The sad fact, however, is that many Christians look to the world for their identity, and they conclude that they are poor or lacking in some way.

The world bases its conclusions upon *comparison*, and if you compare yourself to others you will lose, because you can always find somebody who has more or achieves more than you do. God never calls us to compare ourselves to others. He calls us to look to Christ Jesus, and He says to us, "You are in Christ. There is no comparison to those who are in Christ. You have it *all*—not only now, but forever. Anything of lasting value, anything of great worth, I have given you in Christ Jesus. You have all of Him, and He has all of anything that truly matters!"

The Spirit Himself bears witness with our spirit that we are children of God, and if children, then heirs—heirs of God and joint heirs with Christ, if indeed we suffer with Him, that we may also be glorified together.

—Romans 8:16-17

Why does Paul include suffering in our inheritance with Christ? What sufferings were part of Christ's inheritance?

How can this knowledge that suffering is part of our inheritance help you understand your true identity?

The Nature of Our Inheritance

The Scriptures are very specific about our inheritance in Christ Jesus. Many things are promised to those who are *in Christ*, but in this lesson, we are going to focus on three specific things.

1. We Shall Be Like Christ

Adults often look at children and conclude, "He has his father's genes. He is going to look just like his father when he grows up," or "She has her mother's eyes. She's going to be a beauty just like her mom when she's an adult." We inherit our physical characteristics and attributes from our parents. Similarly, we are destined to mature into the very likeness of Christ Jesus. One day we are going to be *like Him*. 1 John 3:1–2 states:

> Behold what manner of love the Father has bestowed on us, that we should be called children of God! Therefore the world does not know us, because it did not know Him. Beloved, now we are children of God; and it has not yet been revealed what we shall be, but we know that when He is revealed, we shall be like Him, for we shall see Him as He is.

Ask yourself, "What did Christ desire that He did not have?" Nothing! "What did Christ want to do that He was incapable of doing?" Nothing! "What did Christ long to possess that He could not possess?" Nothing! To be like Christ is to have all that Christ has, to know all that Christ knows, to desire all that Christ desires.

For whom He foreknew, He also predestined to be conformed to the image of His Son, that He might be the firstborn among many brethren.

—Romans 8:29

🔊 What does it mean to be "conformed to the image" of Jesus?

🔊 What aspects of Christ's character do you see in your own life? How can this influence your sense of identity?

2. We Will Reign With Christ

Not only will we be like Christ, but we will also rule with Christ. Paul wrote in Ephesians 2:6 that God, in His mercy and because of His great love, has made us alive together with Christ; and then he said that God "raised us up together, and made us sit together in the heavenly places in Christ Jesus." Christ is sitting on His throne in heaven today and, in the spiritual realm, as a believer in Christ you are sitting with Him!

Now a young prince who is crowned king may not receive the *fullness* of his authority as king until he reaches a certain age; nevertheless, he is the crowned king. The years between the time of his coronation and his assumption of full power are years of growing preparation and increasing authority. This is true for our inheritance to "reign with Christ." We have been crowned "joint heir" with Christ and, as we mature in Christ Jesus, our authority and understanding and ability to rule increase. The fullness of our ability to rule begins now, but it ends in eternity.

Ask yourself, "Was there any force of evil or power of the devil that was beyond the ability of Jesus to rule over it?" No! Was any disease greater than the power of Jesus to heal it? No! Was any demon in a person more powerful than Jesus' power to cast it out? No! Was Satan himself more powerful than Jesus? No! Christ in us makes us *more than conquerors* (see Romans 8:37).

❧ What experiences in your own life might God be using to prepare you to reign with Christ?

> Yet in all these things we are more than conquerors through
> Him who loved us.
>
> —Romans 8:37

❧ What does it mean to be "more than conquerors"? What does a conqueror do? What will you do one day, when Christ has resumed His rightful throne?

3. We Will Have a Heavenly Home With Christ

To have the character and nature of Christ, to reign over all things with Christ—what a great inheritance we have been given! Ultimately, of course, we also have the great inheritance of heaven itself. Jesus said, "I go to prepare a place for you. And if I go and prepare a place for you, I will come again and receive you to Myself; that where I am, there you may be also" (John 14:2–3). To be with Christ forever is our greatest inheritance of all. Our inherited "family home" is one in which:

> "God will wipe away every tear from their eyes; there shall be no more death, nor sorrow, nor crying. There shall be no more pain, for the former things have passed away" ... And he showed me a pure river of water of life, clear as crystal, proceeding from the throne of God and of the Lamb. In the middle of its street, and on either side of the river, was the tree of life, which bore twelve fruits, each tree yielding its fruit every month. And the leaves of the tree were for the healing of the nations. And there shall be no more curse, but the throne of God and of the Lamb shall be in it, and His servants shall serve Him. They shall see His face, and His name shall be on their foreheads. There shall be no night there: They need no lamp nor light of the sun, for the Lord God gives them light. And they shall reign forever and ever.
>
> —Revelation 21:4; 22:1–5

Blessed be the God and Father of our Lord Jesus Christ, who according to His abundant mercy has begotten us again to a living hope through the resurrection of Jesus Christ from the dead, to an inheritance incorruptible and undefiled and that does not fade away, reserved in heaven for you.

> —1 Peter 1:3-4

✎ Define each of these elements in your own words:

Incorruptible:

Undefiled:

Does not fade away:

✎ How do these aspects of your inheritance compare with earthly inheritances?

The Guarantee of Our Full Inheritance

How can we be assured that we *are* heirs? How can we be certain that we will receive the full inheritance that God has for us? Paul writes in Ephesians 1:13–14, "You were sealed with the Holy Spirit of promise, who is the guarantee of our inheritance until the redemption of the purchased possession, to the praise of His glory." The Holy Spirit dwelling within us is the proof that God has given us a glorious inheritance and that He is going to bring that inheritance to full fruition in us.

Seals in Bible times were used to indicate four things:

1. *Ownership.* Valuable possessions were protected in containers to which a seal of ownership was attached. We are owned by Christ Jesus, purchased by the price of His shed blood.

2. *Authenticity.* Seals verified that an article was genuine. When the Holy Spirit indwells us, He changes our nature to give authenticity to the truth that Christ Jesus is our Savior and Lord.

3. *Authority.* Official scrolls of kings were sealed to indicate that the documents were backed by the full authority of the king's power and wealth. We are under the authority of God the Father, Son, and Holy Spirit—we are no longer under the authority of the devil.

4. *Completed transactions.* Documents were sealed to indicate that a transaction was complete and established in law. Paul stated repeatedly that we *have* obtained an inheritance in Christ. The transaction of our inheritance was fully completed in Christ's death and resurrection.

What can break what God seals? Nothing. Who can undo what the Holy Spirit does? No one. As believers in Christ Jesus, we are sealed forever "according to the good pleasure of His will, to the praise of the glory of His grace" (Ephesians 1:5–6).

The work of the Holy Spirit brings us to the point of *receiving* our full inheritance. It is nothing that we can achieve or do. It is *His* power that is effective in bringing us to the fullness of Christ's character, authority, and wisdom. It is *His* power that resurrects us to eternal life. Our part is to trust God, to read God's Word, and to listen to the Holy Spirit day by day, and to *obey* what we believe God is calling us to do. It is in this way that we will become the person that God has designed us to be.

The work of the Holy Spirit prepares us to use our inheritance wisely and for the glory of God, accomplished in His timing and according to His methods.

> ...He who has begun a good work in you will complete it until the day of Jesus Christ.
>
> —Philippians 1:6

❧ Why does Paul say that God will complete the "good work" *until* the day of Jesus Christ? Why not *on* that day, or *before* it?

❧ How does this continuing process of God's work affect your view of yourself?

❧ Today and Tomorrow ❧

TODAY: MY INHERITANCE IS TO BE LIKE CHRIST, AND TO REIGN WITH HIM FOREVER.

TOMORROW: I WILL ASK GOD TO TEACH ME HOW TO LIVE LIKE JESUS MORE AND MORE.

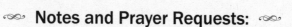

❧ Notes and Prayer Requests: ❧

LESSON 7

Enlightened Saint

❧ In This Lesson ☙ ---

LEARNING: WHAT IS MY CALLING?

GROWING: HOW CAN I FIND THE POWER THAT I LACK?

Are you aware that you have been given the mind of Christ? In order for us to reign with Christ, we must have both the heart and mind of Christ. We must think as He thinks and feel as He feels. We must have both His wisdom and His compassion.

The good news of our inheritance is that in Christ, we have inherited the *nature* of Christ—the character traits of His love, joy, peace, patience, goodness, kindness, faithfulness, gentleness, and self-control—and we have been given Christ's ability to make wise decisions and sound judgments.

Paul writes in Ephesians 1:8 that the riches of God's grace abound toward us "in all wisdom and prudence." God has "made known to us the mystery of His will" and given us "the spirit of wisdom and revelation in the knowledge of Him" (Ephesians 1:9; 1:17). Paul's prayer for the Ephesians was that their understanding might be "enlightened; that you may know what is the hope of His calling, what are the riches of the glory of His inheritance in the saints, and what is the exceeding greatness of His power toward us who believe" (Ephesians 1:18–19).

Ask yourself, "What did Christ want to know that He was incapable of knowing?" Nothing! What did Christ desire to understand that He could not understand? Nothing! What remained a mystery to Christ about God the Father? Nothing!

A child grows in his ability to *use* all of the brain cells that he is given at birth, and in the same way we grow in our ability to understand the deeper things of God *as we grow in our relationship with Christ Jesus.* Our inheritance is to have the *mind* of Christ!

What passages of Scripture did you once understand differently than you do now? How has your understanding deepened as you have grown in Christ?

> And do not be conformed to this world, but be transformed by the renewing of your mind, that you may prove what is that good and acceptable and perfect will of God.
>
> —Romans 12:2

How does a person renew his mind? How does such a renewal enable us to "prove" God's "perfect will"?

Three Things that We are to Know

Paul identified three things that the believer is to know with an "over-flowing understanding": the hope of His calling, the riches of the glory of Christ's inheritance in the saints, and the exceeding greatness of Christ's power. In this lesson we are going to look at each of these areas in which we are privileged to experience "enlightenment."

1. The Hope of His Calling on Our Lives

Many people say, "I'm not called to be a minister." Most of these people believe that only those who are in full-time ministry service are "called." The fact is, each of us is called to be a minister, people who meet the spiritual, emotional, and physical needs of others. To minister is to pray, to listen, to give wise counsel, to share God's Word, to love, to bless, to share one's resources, to affirm, to exercise our ministry gifts given to us by the Holy Spirit. Each of us is called to do this!

The Bible gives us three descriptions about our calling as saints.

1. *An upward call.* Paul writes in Philippians 3:13–14, "Brethren, I do not count myself to have apprehended; but one thing I do, forgetting those things which are behind and reaching forward to those things which are ahead, I press toward the goal for the prize of the *upward call* of God in Christ Jesus" (*emphasis added*).

God's call on our lives continually compels us to reach for higher moral standards, higher levels of understanding, higher character traits, higher ethical conduct, higher degrees of spiritual perfection. We are called to grow, develop, and mature in Christ Jesus so that we might be godly servants. God calls us to be the best that we can be.

2. *A holy calling*. Paul wrote to Timothy, "Share with me in the sufferings for the gospel according to the power of God, who has saved us and called us with a *holy calling*, not according to our works, but according to His own purpose and grace which was given to us in Christ Jesus before time began" (2 Timothy 1:8–9, *emphasis added*).

To be holy is to be separated for use by God. It is to be refined and cleansed so that we no longer think like the world or pursue the lusts of the flesh, the lusts of the eyes, or the pride of life. It is to see ourselves as agents of righteousness, infusing the world with God's purpose and God's goodness as "salt" that preserves, heals, and gives zest to life. Our calling is a call to serve God by serving others.

3. *A heavenly calling*. Our calling is to live a godly life that will influence others to accept Christ. Everything that we do as believers in Christ Jesus should bear spiritual fruit and have eternal benefit. In Hebrews 3:1 we read, "Therefore, holy brethren, partakers of the *heavenly calling*, consider the Apostle and High Priest of our confession, Christ Jesus" (*emphasis added*). We are no longer citizens of this world; we are citizens of heaven. Our purpose is to pray that God's will might be done on earth as it is in heaven, and we are to obey the leading of the Holy Spirit so that we might have a part in making God's will a reality on earth.

In this manner, therefore, pray: Our Father in heaven, Hallowed be Your name. Your kingdom come. Your will be done On earth as it is in heaven.

—Matthew 6:9-10

☙ How is God's will carried out in heaven? How does this compare with the way that His will is obeyed on earth?

☙ What part do *you* have in fulfilling this prayer? How does this help to define your true identity?

2. The Riches of the Glory of His Inheritance in the Saints

God desires that we know our *calling* in Christ, and that we have an understanding about who we *are* from God's perspective. Paul wrote in Ephesians 1:18 that he longed for his readers to be enlightened about the "riches of the glory of His inheritance in the saints."

God gives us all that Christ is, has, and does—His nature, His reign, His eternal life. But what does God give to Christ Jesus as *His* inheritance? Us! The Father says to Jesus, in effect, "Look what a wonderful inheritance I have for You. I have Joe and Roger and Billy for You. I have Sue and Marilyn and Katherine for You."

Many Christians have the attitude, "Well, I'm saved and that's enough."
No! You are the inheritance of Christ Jesus. Don't you long to be all
that you can be for *His* sake? Don't you desire to present yourself holy,
an unblemished and spotless bride? Don't you desire to leave behind
all of the "old you" that was in full force before you accepted Christ and
to become all that the "new you" can possibly be?

When we truly catch a glimpse of how God regards us—the rich inheritance of Christ Jesus—we will place a much higher value upon ourselves and upon all those who are saints with us in Christ Jesus.

> Blessed are those who hunger and thirst for righteousness, For
> they shall be filled.

—Matthew 5:6

List some practical examples of what it means to "hunger
and thirst for righteousness".

How is your appetite for righteousness? What can you do to
hunger and thirst even more?

3. The Greatness of His Power in Us

No believer has justification for saying, "I'm a weakling." As believers in Christ, we have the omnipotent power of God living in us! Paul writes in Ephesians 1:19–23 that he wants his readers to know:

> the exceeding greatness of His power toward us who believe, according to the working of His mighty power which He worked in Christ when He raised Him from the dead and seated Him at His right hand in the heavenly places, far above all principality and power and might and dominion, and every name that is named, not only in this age but also in that which is to come. And He put all things under His feet, and gave Him to be head over all things to the church, which is His body, the fullness of Him who fills all in all.

There is no power greater than that of the Lord who lives in us. The words that Paul used for power reflect energy, strength, and might. The power of the Holy Spirit in us is:

❧ *Resurrection power*. The same power that raised Christ from the dead now resides in you.

❧ *Power over spiritual darkness*. The power within us is greater than that of any force of evil.

❧ *Power over the systems of the world—natural, spiritual, or human*. All things have been put under the feet of Christ.

A little child grows up into the full use of his own physical strength and ability, and we are growing up in our spiritual strength and power in Christ Jesus. Even as we do, we must recognize at all times that the Holy Spirit in us is *greater* than any other form of power that we can ever experience, and that God in us is greater than anything that comes against us (see 1 John 4:4).

How do we activate the power of God in our lives? By waiting on the Lord in quiet trust and by praising God. Waiting on the Lord brings us to a realization of all that He has done for us and all that He is. Praise releases joy into our hearts, and the joy of the Lord *is* our strength.

> "But you shall receive power when the Holy Spirit has come upon you; and you shall be witnesses to Me in Jerusalem, and in all Judea and Samaria, and to the end of the earth."
>
> —Acts 1:8

❧ What "power" does God's Spirit make available to His children?

❧ How can this power in itself be a "witness" to the world around us? How does this influence your identity?

To Know Christ

We are to know our calling, who we are in Christ, and the power of the Holy Spirit in us—but the greatest "knowing" that we can ever have is "knowing Christ." This does not mean knowing *about* Christ, but knowing Christ Himself.

The more we know Christ, the more we know what He wants us to do in every circumstance. In that, we know our calling. The more we know Christ and develop an ever-deepening, intimate relationship with Him, the more we value who He is transforming us to be. In that, we know the richness of our own identity. The more we know Christ and rely upon Him for daily strength and energy, the more we know His power in us. Knowing Christ is the key—not merely knowing *about* Him.

> For this reason I also suffer these things; nevertheless I am not ashamed, for I know whom I have believed and am persuaded that He is able to keep what I have committed to Him until that Day.
>
> —2 Timothy 1:12

❧ What have you committed to Christ for safe keeping?

❧ How does an intimate knowledge of a person help you predict what he will do? How does an intimate knowledge of Jesus help you trust Him for the future?

Our Response to Being Enlightened

Why do we need to know that we are called of God? So that we will have hope about our own future and have a direction for our lives. Why do we need to know that we are the inheritance of Christ Jesus? So that we will begin to reflect the value that God places upon us. Why do we need to know that we have been given exceedingly great power in the Holy Spirit? So that we will act boldly and be courageous in the face of evil, doubt, and persecution.

The good news is that we *must* be enlightened about our position in Christ Jesus, and that we are *given* this wisdom and revelation. God has given us the ability to know, the ability to understand, the ability to discern, the ability to make sound judgments and wise decisions. The things of God are not a mystery to the believer. God wants you to have all the information that you need to live an effective, successful, godly life. He does not play a guessing game with His children. He gives us the wisdom that we need, the power that we need, and the esteem that we need.

> Our part is to read and study God's Word. Our part is to come to God in prayer and to seek a daily, abiding relationship with Him. God's part is to bring His Word to life in our Spirit and to increase our knowledge and understanding. His part is to guide us into the paths of righteousness.

As you read the Scriptures below, make each one a prayer for yourself. Claim by your faith that you truly are an enlightened saint of God!

For God has not given us a spirit of fear, but of power and of love and of a sound mind.

—2 Timothy 1:7

⁓ Give practical examples of how God's Spirit brings you:

Power:

Love:

A sound mind:

⁓ How do these things compare with a spirit of fear? Give practical examples of the spirit of fear which is widespread in the world today.

You are of God, little children, and have overcome them, because He who is in you is greater than he who is in the world.

—1 John 4:4

✍ List below some of the ways in which the Holy Spirit is greater than Satan.

✍ How does having the Holy Spirit within you make you different from when you were a non-Christian? How does this influence your identity now?

✍ Today and Tomorrow ✍

TODAY: I HAVE BEEN CALLED TO SHARE IN CHRIST'S INHERITANCE *AND* TO SHOW FORTH GOD'S POWER.

TOMORROW: I WILL SPEND TIME THIS WEEK IN PRAYER AND BIBLE READING, STRIVING TO KNOW CHRIST BETTER.

LESSON 8

Member of the Body

❧ In This Lesson ❧

LEARNING: WHERE CAN I FIND LASTING PEACE?

GROWING: WHAT DOES IT MEAN TO BE PART OF THE "BODY OF CHRIST"?

Do you ever question whether you really "fit" anywhere? Do you have a firm understanding that you belong—that you are a full member of Christ's body? Paul writes in Ephesians 1:23 that the church, which is composed of all true believers in Christ Jesus, is "His body, the fullness of Him who fills all in all."

Prior to being a part of the body of Christ, you were an individual, alone and isolated. You were not able to enter into a relationship with God, and you were not capable of having an eternal, fully reconciled relationship with another human being. "But," you may say, "people who aren't in Christ fall in love, get married, make friends, and are in relationship with other people." Yes—but only at a surface level. Without genuine forgiveness and love, no person can truly enter into an abiding, deep relationship with another person. Our abilities to forgive and to express love are always drawn ultimately from our having received forgiveness and love from God. Only the believer experiences such forgiveness and love.

Those who are separate from Christ are separate from God and from believers. Those who are in Christ are no longer separated from God or other believers; they are united together as *one body.*

Paul describes this reconciliation in Ephesians 2:11–13:

> Therefore remember that you, once Gentiles in the flesh—who are called Uncircumcision by what is called the Circumcision made in the flesh by hands—that at that time you were without Christ, being aliens from the commonwealth of Israel and strangers from the covenants of promise, having no hope and without God in the world. But now in Christ Jesus you who once were far off have been brought near by the blood of Christ.

To be "brought near" by the blood of Christ means to enter into an intimate relationship with God and to be fully "accepted in the Beloved" as Paul wrote earlier in his epistle. (See Ephesians 1:6.) To be "brought near" is also a Jewish term relating to the Temple.

The courts of the temple were arranged so that the "court of the Gentiles" was the farthest court from the Holy of Holies, which held the ark of the covenant and was the seat of God's presence among the Israelites. The next court was the court of the righteous Jewish women, and the next was the court of the righteous Jewish men. The inner court was reserved for those who served as priests before God.

In Christ, believers are brought into the very presence of God—regardless of whether they were originally Jews or Gentiles. Belief in Christ Jesus brings us into the direct presence of God Almighty. Furthermore, Jesus taught that we, as believers in Him, are united completely with Him and with the Father. He prayed for us the night that He prayed for His disciples:

I do not pray for these alone, but also for those who will believe in Me through their word; that they all may be one, as You, Father, are in Me, and I in You; that they also may be one in Us, that the world may believe that You sent me. And the glory which You gave Me I have given them, that they may be one just as We are one: I in them, and You in Me; that they may be made perfect in one, and that the world may know that You have sent Me, and have loved them as You have loved Me.

—John 17:20–23

❧ How do you feel, knowing that Jesus was praying specifically for *you* before going to the cross?

❧ Consider how closely linked Jesus is to God the Father. How does it affect you to realize that you, also, are as closely linked to the Body of Christ?

Peace Within the Body

The key word that Paul uses in describing our new identity of belonging to the body of Christ is *peace*. He writes in Ephesians 2:14–19:

> For He Himself is our peace, who has made both one, and has broken down the middle wall of separation, having abolished in His flesh the enmity, that is, the law of commandments contained in ordinances, so as to create in Himself one new man from the two, thus making peace, and that He might reconcile them both to God in one body through the cross, thereby putting to death the enmity. And He came and preached peace to you who were afar off and to those who were near. For through Him we both have access by one Spirit to the Father. Now, therefore, you are no longer strangers and foreigners, but fellow citizens with the saints and members of the household of God.

Our ability to be at peace with other people flows from Christ, who abides in us as Peacemaker. No law can ever force two people to be at peace with each other. No peace treaty can ever bring about lasting peace unless all parties have peace in their hearts toward one another.

Again and again, we see worldly peace treaties erupt into war, because what was drafted on paper had not been written first on the hearts of the people. Again and again, we find individuals claiming that they are at peace with each other, only to see the peace shattered by arguments and hostile attitudes. This is because the peace which they claimed was only on the surface—it was not a true peace in their hearts.

Christ alone makes lasting and genuine peace possible. It is when we recognize and accept Christ's peace within that we can enter into a ministry of reconciliation with others. A ministry of reconciliation means that we become peacemakers ourselves—speaking God's peace to those who are sinners and inviting them to enter a reconciled relationship with God. We also speak peace to our fellow believers, that we all might become fully united in the Spirit.

❧ What relationships have changed in your own life since becoming a Christian? When have you become reconciled with someone that you didn't like previously?

> Now all things are of God, who has reconciled us to Himself through Jesus Christ, and has given us the ministry of reconciliation, that is, that God was in Christ reconciling the world to Himself, not imputing their trespasses to them, and has committed to us the word of reconciliation.
>
> —2 Corinthians 5:18-19

❧ What exactly is "the ministry of reconciliation"? Who has exercised that ministry in your life?

❧ What does it mean that God was "not imputing their trespasses to them"? How have you benefited from this? What people in your own life need this from you?

We Are God's Temple

One of the great illustrations that Paul uses to describe the body of Christ is that of a temple. He writes in Ephesians 2:19–22 that his readers were members of the...

> ...household of God, having been built on the foundation of the apostles and prophets, Jesus Christ Himself being the chief cornerstone, in whom the whole building, being joined together, grows into a holy temple in the Lord, in whom you also are being built together for a dwelling place of God in the Spirit.

The Ephesians were living in the shadow of a great temple to the pagan goddess Diana, one of the seven wonders of the ancient world. This temple was built to bring "glory" to the goddess Diana. The Greeks thought that the god or goddess that had the greatest temple was the god or goddess with the most importance, and the most important god or goddess would surely reside in the most important city on earth. The Ephesians claimed that place of preeminence for themselves because of the temple to Diana.

Paul used this as a springboard for a deeper teaching about the identity of the believer. He said, "You are a holy temple in the Lord." He saw the believers as a dwelling place of God in the spirit—a magnificent temple that was not made with human hands but that was created by Christ Jesus. This temple is eternal. It is magnificent because it is the work of Christ. And it is a temple that is ever growing—more and more believers are simply making it a more and more glorious temple.

Finally, this temple of believers is intended for one purpose—to reflect the *glory of God*. It is not intended to draw attention or praise to the believers, either individually or as a group, but to focus faith, hope, and love upon the One who created it—the Lord God Almighty!

Do you not know that you are the temple of God and that the
Spirit of God dwells in you?

—1 Corinthians 3:16

❧ What does it mean that "you are the temple of God"? How, in
specific terms, should this affect your life?

❧ What effect does God's Spirit have on your identity? On your
purpose within the Body of Christ?

Many Functions, One Body

In being united to other believers in Christ's body, we do not lose our
individual identity. Rather, we have the blessed opportunity to express
our individual identity and gifts in cooperation with other believers.
We are not all the same within the body of Christ—rather, we are united into one purpose.

Paul wrote about this very clearly in Romans 12:4–8:

> For as we have many members in one body, but all the members do not have the same function, so we, being many, are one body in Christ, and individually members of one another. Having then gifts differing according to the grace that is given to us, let us use them: if prophecy, let us prophesy in proportion to our faith; or ministry, let us use it in our ministering; he who teaches, in teaching; he who exhorts, in exhortation; he who gives, with liberality; he who leads, with diligence; he who shows mercy, with cheerfulness.

We are to give our gifts in acts of ministry and open ourselves up to receiving the ministry gifts of other believers, so that we might be made whole *as a body* and so we might grow in our ability to love God and love others.

> ...but, speaking the truth in love, [we] may grow up in all things into Him who is the head—Christ—from whom the whole body, joined and knit together by what every joint supplies, according to the effective working by which every part does its share, causes growth of the body for the edifying of itself in love.

> —Ephesians 4:15-16

🕊 What does Paul mean when he says that "every part does its share" within the Body of Christ? What is *your* share in the growth of the Body?

97

What does Paul say is the whole purpose of the Body's growth? How is love essential to the Body's health?

Our Life as His Body

How can the body of Christ function if the body is scattered and divided? How can the body of Christ function unless believers come together and worship the Lord and minister to one another? Again and again, the writers of the New Testament call us to be involved with one another. We are part of a living entity—the body of Christ. We are intended to be in close relationship and to function together as a whole. Read what the writers of the Bible have said:

And let us consider one another in order to stir up love and good works, not forsaking the assembling of ourselves together, as is the manner of some, but exhorting one another, and so much the more as you see the Day approaching.

—Hebrews 10:24-25

And do not be drunk with wine, in which is dissipation; but be filled with the Spirit, speaking to one another in psalms and hymns and spiritual songs, singing and making melody in your heart to the Lord, giving thanks always for all things to God the Father in the name of our Lord Jesus Christ, submitting to one another in the fear of God.

—Ephesians 5:18-21

Confess your trespasses to one another, and pray for one another, that you may be healed. The effective, fervent prayer of a righteous man avails much.

—James 5:16

Therefore comfort each other and edify one another, just as you also are doing.

—1 Thessalonians 5:11

☙ Read through these verses and underline every use of "other" and "one another". What central theme is present in all these passages?

☙ Consider the analogy of the human body as representing all Christians. Why is it so important that Christians consider "one another" in every way?

Our function as members of Christ's body is three-fold: to build up the body of Christ, to create a sense of belonging for all believers, and to bring glory to the Lord. If we have an identity as part of the body of Christ, we will do everything possible to function as part of the body. And in functioning as His body, we grow in our own sense of belonging and enjoy reconciliation and fellowship with others.

> For as we have many members in one body, but all the members do not have the same function, so we, being many, are one body in Christ, and individually members of one another.

> —Romans 12:4-5

❧ What does it mean that Christians are "members of one another"? Give specific examples of how you have seen this in practice.

❧ What "body part" are you most like in the Body of Christ?

Today and Tomorrow

TODAY: BEING A PART OF THE BODY OF CHRIST MEANS THAT I MUST *DO* MY PART, BEING AT PEACE WITH OTHERS.

TOMORROW: I WILL ASK THE LORD TO TEACH ME MORE FULLY WHAT MY PART IS WITHIN HIS BODY.

Notes and Prayer Requests:

Lesson 9

Holy Vessel for Ministry

──────── ❧ **In This Lesson** ☙ ────────

LEARNING: WHAT IS MY PURPOSE IN LIFE?

GROWING: HOW CAN I LEARN TO DO GOOD WORKS?

──────── ❧☙ ────────

As believers in Christ Jesus, we are members of a *living* body. In a very practical way, we are the "hands and feet" of the Lord on the earth today. Christ works through our hands to touch a sick person, clothe a naked person, and hand a cup of cold water to a thirsty person. Christ walks with our feet into areas of need. Christ speaks through our mouths His words of comfort and edification.

We have a great and glorious purpose on earth: we are to be agents of God's love, ambassadors for Christ, the initiators of good works. We are to pour out our lives in service to others, just as Christ gave Himself for us. Paul writes in Ephesians 5:1–2, "Be imitators of God as dear children. And walk in love, as Christ also has loved us and given Himself for us, an offering and a sacrifice to God for a sweet-smelling aroma."

Works can never save us, purchase our forgiveness, or qualify us to receive God's love, yet good works are the natural outcome of our salvation. Once we have been born again, our natural impulse is toward good works. Paul also wrote in Ephesians 5:8–10, "For you were once darkness, but now you are light in the Lord. Walk as children of light (for the fruit of the Spirit is in all goodness, righteousness, and truth), finding out what is acceptable to the Lord."

Jesus walked this earth healing the sick and brokenhearted, preaching good tidings to the poor, proclaiming liberty to the captives, giving hope to the oppressed, and comforting those who mourn. We are to follow in His footsteps and do the same. Jesus calls and commissions us to His ministry, just as He commissioned the disciples:

> And He called the twelve to Himself, and began to send them out two by two, and gave them power over unclean spirits ... So they went out and preached that people should repent. And they cast out many demons, and anointed with oil many who were sick, and healed them.

> —Mark 6:7, 12–13

What power did the disciples have which enabled them to cast out demons and heal the sick?

List two or three people below that you know who are sick or discouraged. How can you minister to them this week?

103

Created for Good Works

Paul writes in Ephesians 2:10 that we have been "created in Christ Jesus for good works, which God prepared beforehand that we should walk in them." God made you with a purpose in mind—He has had a plan for your life from before the foundation of the world, a plan that you are uniquely designed to fulfill. The Lord knows precisely the good works that you are capable of doing, and also those which you will excel in doing, which will give you a great sense of satisfaction.

ℝ When have you known that you were doing precisely what God had created you to do? What was it? What were the results?

A "good work" is any work that reflects Jesus and brings glory to God. *Good* is the same word that God used in evaluating each aspect of creation: "And God saw that it was good" (Genesis 1:10, 12, 18, 25). The creative work of God is not finished. It is ongoing by the power of the Holy Spirit in your life and mine. God continues to shine light into darkness, to bring forth good out of evil, order out of confusion, and purpose out of things that seem meaningless. One of the best-known verses in all the Bible declares, "All things work together for good to those who love God, to those who are the called according to His purpose" (Romans 8:28). No matter what happens to us or around us, the Holy Spirit is capable of producing a "good work" in us and through us!

But be doers of the word, and not hearers only, deceiving yourselves. For if anyone is a hearer of the word and not a doer, he
is like a man observing his natural face in a mirror; for he ob-
serves himself, goes away, and immediately forgets what kind
of man he was.

—James 1:22-24

❧ When you see your reflection in a mirror, what features are
you most likely to concentrate on? What sorts of "primping" do
you do?

❧ How do we deceive ourselves if we are "hearers only" of God's
word? What does it mean to be a "doer of the word"?

⌒∞⌒ No Room for an Inferiority Complex ⌒∞⌒

Many Christians say about themselves, "I'm not capable of ministry." The fact is, none of us are capable by ourselves. But with Christ, all things are possible. As Paul in Philippians 4:13, "I can do all things through Christ who strengthens me."

God supplies to us what we are lacking. When we are weak, He gives us the strength to be strong. When we are without resources, He supplies the resources. When we are without courage, He gives us the ability to endure and to be bold. Again and again in the Bible we have examples of those who *could not* in their own ability, but who *could* as they received the strength of the Lord.

Paul wrote about a painful "thorn in the flesh" that the Lord did not remove from his life, even though he had prayed repeatedly that it be removed. He told the Corinthians how the Lord had said to him, "My grace is sufficient for you, for My strength is made perfect in weakness." Paul concluded, "Therefore most gladly I will rather boast in my infirmities, that the power of Christ may rest upon me. Therefore I take pleasure in infirmities, in reproaches, in needs, in persecutions, in distresses, for Christ's sake. For when I am weak, then I am strong" (2 Corinthians 12:9–10).

And God is able to make all grace abound toward you, that you, always having all sufficiency in all things, may have an abundance for every good work.

—2 Corinthians 9:8

🔖 Why do we need "an abundance" of grace "for every good work"? What does God's grace have to do with our good works?

🔖 How does the calling to good works influence your identity?

Our Identity As His Witnesses

We are created for good works, and we are called to be Christ's witnesses. We are to proclaim the good news of His death and resurrection—and to be bold in telling others about God's love, mercy, grace, and free offer of forgiveness and eternal life. We have a "good message" to accompany our "good works"!

Peter and John were put in prison and then called before the religious leaders in Jerusalem and threatened for proclaiming that Jesus was the Christ. They answered, "We cannot but speak the things which we have seen and heard" (Acts 4:20). Peter and John were released with further threats, and they returned to their fellow believers. After they had told all that had happened to them, the disciples prayed this: "Now, Lord, look on their threats, and grant to Your servants that with all boldness they may speak Your word" (Acts 4:29). What was the result? "They spoke the word of God with boldness" and the "multitude of those who believed were of one heart and one soul" (Acts 4:31–32).

"Go therefore and make disciples of all the nations, baptizing them in the name of the Father and of the Son and of the Holy Spirit, teaching them to observe all things that I have commanded you; and lo, I am with you always, even to the end of the age." Amen.

—Matthew 28:19-20

❧ Jesus commands His followers to teach others "to observe all things that I have commanded you". What is required of you if you are to teach that to others?

❧ How does this responsibility affect your self-identity?

Our Identity As His Ambassadors

We are God's ambassadors when we are doing good works and proclaiming the "good news" of Christ. As Paul writes in 2 Corinthians 5:20, "We are ambassadors for Christ, as though God were pleading through us." We are citizens of heaven, sojourning on this earth in temporary "tents"—our physical bodies. We are "fellow citizens with the saints" who have gone before us (see Ephesians 2:19). Our true home is in heaven.

When we see ourselves as citizens of an everlasting kingdom—only temporarily on this earth to speak the "good news" of Christ and to do good works—we will have a new perspective on our possessions, our commitments and agendas, and our use of time and resources. Our priorities will change. No longer will we see ourselves as needing to accomplish man-made goals; no longer will we cling to material things; no longer will we feel the need to get ahead and achieve fame and power in the eyes of the world. When we have a firm identity that we are citizens of heaven, ambassadors for Christ on earth, we will make the most of our earthly time and resources for eternal reward!

Do you truly see yourself today as a vessel of God intended for His purposes of ministry on this earth—purposes that involve doing good works and proclaiming the good news? Ask the Lord to help you see yourself as He sees you. Many Christians think that, once they are saved, the rest of their lives is a long, slow slide through life until they land in eternity. Not so! We have work to do and a message to proclaim. And today is the day for doing what God has called us to do!

> "Do not lay up for yourselves treasures on earth, where moth and rust destroy and where thieves break in and steal; but lay up for yourselves treasures in heaven, where neither moth nor rust destroys and where thieves do not break in and steal. For where your treasure is, there your heart will be also."

—Matthew 6:19-21

ᴥ What do you treasure most in life? What things are honestly of the greatest value to you?

ᴥ What does it mean to "lay up treasures in heaven"? What sorts of treasure can you "lay up" for eternity? How do you accomplish that?

Even so, every good tree bears good fruit, but a bad tree bears bad fruit. A good tree cannot bear bad fruit, nor can a bad tree bear good fruit. Every tree that does not bear good fruit is cut down and thrown into the fire.

—Matthew 7:17-19

❧ What sorts of "fruit" is your life bearing? Write two columns below and give specific examples of good fruit and bad fruit.

❧ What will you do this week to increase the "good fruit" column? To decrease the "bad fruit" column?

❧ Today and Tomorrow ❧

TODAY: I AM CALLED TO BE BOTH A WITNESS AND AN AMBASSADOR FOR CHRIST TO THE WORLD AROUND ME.

TOMORROW: I WILL CULTIVATE GOOD FRUIT IN MY LIFE AND CUT OUT THE BAD FRUIT.

LESSON 10

God's Masterpiece

─────── ❧ **In This Lesson** ❧ ───────

LEARNING: WHAT DOES IT MEAN TO BE COMPLETE IN CHRIST?

GROWING: HOW CAN I CHANGE FROM BEING A MESS TO A MASTERPIECE?

✧

Are you aware that you are God's masterpiece? Paul writes in Ephesians 2:10, "We are His workmanship." The word *workmanship* has been translated also as "masterpiece." We are God's supreme "work in progress"—a work that will culminate in perfection.

A masterpiece is a work of notable excellence. From the first chapter of the Bible we see that God considered man to be the crowning achievement of His creation. Of all God's creatures, only man was made in the image of God—only man was made capable of spiritual growth and development, of reasoning, of faith, of learning concepts and principles, of making sound decisions and wise judgments, of planning for a future and remembering the details of the past. God breathed into man His own breath, His essence, His presence. God gave man a will with which to discern good from evil and to choose between them.

It makes a great difference whether you see yourself as a mess or a masterpiece. If you believe that you are worthless, without potential and without any hope of excellence, you are likely to give up, become dejected, and become "sick of life." On the other hand, if you believe that you are a masterpiece in the making, with vast potential for excellence, you are going to have hope, enthusiasm for life, and a desire to pursue all that God has for you!

✎ Rate your own self-image on a scale of 1 to 10, where 1 = "I'm worthless," 10 = "I'm flawless," and 5 = "God is making me in His image."

God's Plan: Our Perfection

As we have stated repeatedly in this Bible study, we are believers *in Christ*. Christ Himself is our identity. Here is what Paul said about Christ: "He [Christ] is the image of the invisible God" (Colossians 1:15). Jesus Christ was the appearance of God in human form so that we might see the perfection of God in a human likeness to which we could relate fully.

If we are *in Christ*, we are to reflect the perfection of God in human form. As Paul writes in Colossians 1:19, "For it pleased the Father that in Him all the fullness should dwell." Jesus Christ was the *begotten* Son of God. From the moment of His birth He was a perfect reflection of God's nature. We are the *born-again, in-the-process-of-becoming-perfect* children of God. From the moment of our spiritual rebirth, the Holy Spirit indwells us and begins to grow us to reflect Christ's nature.

Our future *is* that we will be like Christ. We will be perfect, whole, complete—just as He is perfect, whole, and complete. God's plan for our lives is to lead us to perfection, wholeness, completion, and fullness. As you read through the verses below, note the theme of God's bringing us to a perfect reflection of Himself.

> ...He who has begun a good work in you will complete it until the day of Jesus Christ.

> —Philippians 1:6

> Therefore you shall be perfect, just as your Father in heaven is perfect.

> —Matthew 5:48

> ...Become complete. Be of good comfort, be of one mind, live in peace; and the God of love and peace will be with you.

> —2 Corinthians 13:11

> All Scripture is given by inspiration of God, and is profitable for doctrine, for reproof, for correction, for instruction in righteousness, that the man of God may be complete, thoroughly equipped for every good work.

> —2 Timothy 3:16-17

> Now may the God of peace who brought up our Lord Jesus from the dead, that great Shepherd of the sheep, through the blood of the everlasting covenant, make you complete in every good work to do His will, working in you what is well pleasing in His sight, through Jesus Christ, to whom be glory forever and ever. Amen.

> —Hebrews 13:20-21

☙ Go through these verses and make a list below of all the things involved in making us "complete" and "perfect".

☙ What is God's part in making you complete? What is your part?

What a glorious future lies ahead for us! But note that, in each of the verses above, it is God who does the sanctifying, cleansing, and perfecting work in us—by His Word and by His presence, He is the One who *makes* us whole. Our perfection is not something which we can achieve or should strive to achieve. Our perfection is not of our own doing—we are *His* workmanship.

The Perfecting Process

The process of our perfection may at times be painful. It is God who chisels us, sands us, molds us. It is God who sometimes chooses to bring us into difficult situations so that we might deepen our reliance upon Him and grow in our relationship with Him. As it says in Jeremiah 18:1–6, we are clay in His hands:

> The word which came to Jeremiah from the LORD, saying: "Arise and go down to the potter's house, and there I will cause you to hear My words." Then I went down to the potter's house, and there he was, making something at the wheel. And the vessel that he made of clay was marred in the hand of the potter; so he made it again into another vessel, as it seemed good to the potter to make. Then the word of the LORD came to me, saying: "O house of Israel, can I not do with you as this potter?" says the LORD. "Look, as the clay is in the potter's hand, so are you in My hand."

 When have you felt that the Lord was "remaking" you on His potter's wheel?

 How does Jeremiah's potter illustrate the Lord's work in your own life? How does this "vessel in the making" image affect your identity?

∞ A Cleansing Process ∞

I have had the opportunity to visit some of the famous art galleries and museums in the world, and I like to look for my favorite paintings. In one museum, I noticed that a particular painting was missing, and I asked a guide if it had been sold to another museum. He responded, "No, it is out being cleaned." From time to time, God removes us from the spotlight so that He might cleanse something from our lives. His perfecting work is removing impurities from our lives so that we might more perfectly reflect Him.

> "But who can endure the day of His coming? And who can stand when He appears? For He is like a refiner's fire And like launderers' soap. He will sit as a refiner and a purifier of silver; He will purify the sons of Levi, And purge them as gold and silver, That they may offer to the LORD An offering in righteousness."
>
> —Malachi 3:2-3

∞ Silver and gold are refined with very hot flames, and launderer's soap is harsh. What does this suggest about God's process of purifying His children?

∞ According to these verses, why does God purify us? What new insight does this give to your self-identity?

Believing God for Perfection

God alone does the work of perfecting us—of making us, remaking us, refining us—so what is our part? Our part is to *receive by faith what God is doing in our lives*. We are to take God at His Word and trust Him to do His work in us, opening ourselves to His work, inviting His work in us, and believing that God is at work even when we can't see the results. He is always behind the scenes of our lives, turning all things toward an eternal benefit for us. We are His workmanship. He never removes His grace from our lives. He never withdraws or takes His hand off of us. We are always in His everlasting arms. What God begins, God completes.

Trust in the LORD with all your heart, And lean not on your own understanding; In all your ways acknowledge Him, And He shall direct your paths.

—Proverbs 3:5-6

Give practical examples of when you have leaned on your own understanding in the past. What were the results?

What does it mean to "acknowledge" God in all your ways? How is this done practically?

Taking God at His Word

It is God who says that, the moment you receive Jesus Christ as your Savior, you are *in Christ*. It is God who says that He chose you, He loves you, He has redeemed you from the bondage of sin, and that He has forgiven you and changed your sin nature. It is God who declares that you are His heir, an enlightened saint with the mind of Christ, a member of the body of Christ, and a holy vessel in His hands. It is God who declares that you are His masterpiece.

The real question facing us today is this: Will you believe what God says about you? Will you take Him at His word, by faith, and trust Him to do His work in you?

...let us lay aside every weight, and the sin which so easily en-snares us, and let us run with endurance the race that is set before us, looking unto Jesus, the author and finisher of our faith, who for the joy that was set before Him endured the cross, despising the shame, and has sat down at the right hand of the throne of God.

—Hebrews 12:1-2

∾ What "race" has been set for you this week? What sort of endurance is the Lord asking of you?

∾ According to these verses, what motivated Jesus to go to the cross? How can you find that same motivation in "running the race" for Christ?

❧ Today and Tomorrow ❧

TODAY: GOD IS AT WORK IN MY LIFE, MAKING ME INTO A PERFECT REFLECTION OF HIS SON.

TOMORROW: I WILL WORK TOGETHER WITH GOD IN PURIFYING AND PERFECTING THAT IMAGE.

❧ Notes and Prayer Requests: ❧

∞ Notes and Prayer Requests: ∞